CONNECTICUT,

formerly the

CONSTITUTION STATE

---

*How the Politicians and Judges have
Subjugated the Citizen to the State*

PETER THALHEIM

PAGE PUBLISHING
Conneaut Lake, PA

Contents

Introduction

As a Nutmegger, I used to be able to take pride in the fact that Connecticut was the Constitution State! It is right there on our license plates and has been there since I was a kid. I cannot say that I was always a Nutmegger as we immigrated here from West Germany when I was just turning three. But going to K-12 in the public schools certainly gave me some reason to consider myself a native. I know the routine in Vermont and Maine: if you weren't born there, you are not actually a Vermonter or Mainer. I haven't come across that prejudice in Connecticut, however, in my five decades here.

So what does it mean to be the Constitution State? New Hampshire has one of my favorites: "Live free or die." You may recall that slogan from your history or social studies class in school? That was one of the battle cries and slogans during the Revolutionary War of Independence after 1775. There were also flags that showed a snake and said, "Don't tread on me." That was first used by politician and General Christopher Gadsen in 1775 during the American Revolution. The rattlesnake usually won't seek you out to tangle with you, but if you provoke the rattlesnake, the rattlesnake will come back with a very tough bite! So beware. We are ready to defend our freedoms. In fact, this flag of "Don't tread on me" partially motivated my gubernatorial campaign design in 2017–2018 that showed a python squeezing the State of Connecticut to death. My snake was not one of independence and resilience; instead, my python represented the administrative state in Connecticut and how the administrative state was squeezing the life out of Connecticut. There are many more regulations, many more regulators, time delays, and required obeisance to the state today that we are working for the state and not for ourselves, the citizens. The result for Connecticut is, people are leaving, talent is leaving, and capital is leaving. *Capital* refers to wealth. Wealth is leaving the state as money is not stupid. *Webster's New World Dictionary* [1] defines *capital* as "3. wealth (money or property) owned or used in business or by a person, corporation, etc… 5. wealth, in whatever form, used or capable of being used to produce assets; resources; as energy and education are his only *capital*…" Just the amount of wealth that has left the state could likely have balanced our budgets if kept here to invest in the Connecticut economy and pay income taxes to the state. But the administrative state and its facilitators, the statists, know no limits! At the bottom of my piece of art was the phrase, "The Administrative State Claims its Victim." And if you took a closer look at the Gold Coast of Connecticut, the towns of Greenwich, Stamford, Darien, New Canaan, Norwalk, Westport, Wilton, and Weston, you would have seen the crossed-out eyes of a dead state. The *CTMirror* was even gracious enough to make the crossed-out eyes darker and more visible to accompany some of my opinion pieces that they were generous enough to run during the campaign.

Funny how some people cannot see what is in front of them. Or, perhaps, they don't want to see what is in front of them. The *Hartford Courant,* one of the great facilitators of the ruination of Connecticut by the administrative state, could only see the fangs on the python. They pretended that they didn't know the significance of the moment or the message. Better not shed light on the truth that opposes their statist narrative. It would be like looking at the greatest work of art ever produced in the history of man, Michelangelo's *David* in Florence, Italy, and focusing on his sandals or maybe a knot

---

[1]   *College Edition* (Cleveland: The World Publishing Co., 1964), 216.

in his slingshot. Dishonesty. "All The News that's Fit to Print?" Oh, sorry, that's another newspaper.

In New England we have Maine as Vacationland. Rhode Island is the Ocean State. Vermont is the Green Mountain State. Massachusetts is the Spirit of America; formerly, "The spirit of Massachusetts is the spirit of America." Neighboring New York is the Empire State. New Jersey is the Garden State. Pennsylvania is the Keystone State. Virginia is R-rated: "Virginia is for lovers." Texas has some gravitas as the Lone Star State. Colorado—which should not be confused with *Connecticut* as they both begin with a *c*, and they are next to each other in the alphabetical list of the fifty states—has a row of mountains in the background, which is fitting as Colorado has the Rocky Mountains marching through the state. The Continental Divide runs through Colorado. What is the significance of the Continental Divide in our great nation? It is not the polarization between political right and left, but rather that all the water that falls to the west of the slope empties into the Pacific, and all the water that falls on the eastern side empties into the Atlantic.

Chapter 1

The Constitution State and the Rule of Law

As a disinterested observer, I declare that Connecticut has the most significant motto for its license plate: the Constitution State. And since the Rule of Law is the most significant development in the political history of man, our constitution was at the core of the Rule of Law. If Connecticut were still following its own constitution, which it is not, it would be in a much better financial and socioeconomic condition today than it is. That is to say that the key to reigniting Connecticut, and this may apply to your state as well, as a desirable place to go with your family and business requires a reimposition of the principles embodied in the state constitution. It is my opinion after living here for decades and taking a closer look at my state's ailments during the gubernatorial campaign of 2017–2018 that our state no longer has free will and is, instead, controlled by special interests. Our state is not run for the citizenry, but rather for special categories of citizens. But I am getting ahead of myself. What was the significance of the Connecticut constitution to our founding fathers at the time that our national constitution was drafted at the Constitutional Convention in Philadelphia in 1787? The convention had originally been called to improve upon the Articles of Confederation, which dated to after the Declaration of Independence in July 1776. The articles became effective in 1781, but proved to have numerous shortcomings. The Constitutional Convention was to address these shortcomings, but moved on to draft a whole new constitution, something that was beyond the delegates' original mission.

There were basically two different plans that competed for supporters. There was the Virginia Plan that favored large states by population, such as Virginia and New York. The Virginia Plan would have two legislative bodies, but both legislative bodies would be selected by the proportionate size of each state's population. That would mean that a few of the big states could dominate their lesser sisters. These two legislative bodies would also select presidents and appoint judges. The smaller states did not want to be rendered obsolete and drafted a counterproposal for what became the New Jersey Plan. The New Jersey Plan would continue to have one legislative body as they had under the Articles of Confederation with each state having one vote. There would be a multiperson executive. Clearly, one state and one vote would not work for the more populous states as too much authority would be left in small states like Rhode Island and New Hampshire. Totally proportionate representation would not work as just a handful of states could dominate the union through their large population numbers. Well, you know the solution. It was the Great Compromise or, better yet, the Connecticut Compromise. There would be two legislatures. One would be elected based on proportion of population so that the large states could have greater influence, and the other legislature—in our case, the Senate—would have two members elected or appointed by each state. That would allow the smaller states to protect their relevance and sovereignty. The Connecticut Compromise also included a one-person president to be selected by the Electoral College.

Before the Revolution, Connecticut had the General Assembly: "The General Assembly consisted of two houses, the Council and the Assembly. The Council, the more powerful of the two houses, consisted of the ex officio governor and lieutenant governor and a stable number of twelve elected assistants. It provided a model for the Senate. The Council varied in number up to 200 members, with each town sending either one or two representatives. It provided a model for the House of Representatives."[2]

---

[2] "The Crucial Decade: 1780s: History of Connecticut's Contribution to the Federal Constitution," December 6, 2012, social.rollins.edu.

Chapter 2

Connecticut's Preferred Citizens

From such a glorious beginning in the 1700s to our ignominious position today as having one of the worst financial conditions of the fifty states is a sad story. Our state is run by the public unions for themselves and their members and by other special interests. It is a truism to say that the public unions are allied with the Democratic Party, and the Democratic Party cannot, under the present conditions, win without the support of the able public unions. The unions provide much-needed volunteers and contributions to the Democratic Party, and the Democratic Party returns the favor by lavishing pay, benefits, health care, disability compensation, and pension promises on the public unions far above what is offered in the private sector. Connecticut was once a vibrant state, but has been rendered a subsidiary of these vested interests. The Connecticut Supreme Court is of no aid to the common citizen of Connecticut as the Connecticut Supreme Court is peopled by jurists who buy into the public union scheme since most of the jurists owe their political career and position to the machine. They are thorough statists and have forgotten that the Revolution was waged for the citizen to emerge as the sovereign. Instead, our Supreme Court will support the State nine times out of ten if the State is in a contest with the citizen. When the State comes to fine you today; or to rescind your license to conduct your business; or to seize your land to give it to politically favored parties who will enrich themselves and their political allies;

or to withhold a license; or to revoke a license for you to start a business or create a business or maintain a business, the State wins unless there is clear statutory language in favor of the citizen. Even then, the Supreme Court might fall back on the all-purpose jackknife: "Well, we will defer to the government officials' judgment as they are operating a department that has been created by action of the legislature."

The Connecticut Supreme Court has it backward! The citizen is to win in any confrontation with the State nine times out of ten unless the State can point to clear and unequivocal statutory language that supports the State's position. Instead, the statist relies on ever-the-undemocratic bromide that "the statute is remedial in nature; therefore, we will interpret the language liberally to give effect to the broad statutory purpose of the statute." We were taught that as one of the methods of statutory interpretation in law school back in 1982–1985. It sounds reasonable when a law professor proposes it to you. It reads nicely when you read it in court opinions, but it is undemocratic. Under the Ninth Amendment to the Constitution, adopted as part of the original Bill of Rights in 1789, "The enumeration in the Constitution, of certain rights, shall not be construed to deny or disparage others retained by the people."[3] There is also the truism of the Tenth Amendment that "[t]he powers not delegated to the United States by the Constitution, nor prohibited by it to the States, are reserved to the States respectively, or to the people."[4] These Amendments merely reiterate a truism that the federal government received no more rights in the constitution then specifically granted. The point is, if a statute was to mean something, it should say it. But sometimes proposed legislation has specific language removed from it or is never inserted into the proposed legislation because, otherwise, the legislation would go down to legislative defeat. The language passed is the language that was voted on by the legislature. If you add language later by judicial interpretation, then the court is substituting its opinion for the act of a democratically elected legislature! Don't do an end run around the legislature. The way of

---

[3] Amendment IX to the U.S. Constitution.
[4] Amendment X to the U.S. Constitution.

interpreting statutes is to enforce what is actually written in them. This approach is sometimes referred to as a contract theory that the legislation passed is all that can be enforced and not to have additional powers or prohibitions interpreted into it; otherwise, it would not have passed. It was, basically, the contract entered into between the legislators and the governor if the governor signed the legislation.

But back to the original point, Connecticut is no longer operating by free will and has not done so for forty years. This is a direct result of the general citizen never having enough legislators and governor in office at one time to represent the interest of the general citizen versus the special interests. Even when Republicans have occasionally had Republican governors over the past forty years, those governors could not get laws passed to bring the laws back to benefit the general citizen when one or both houses of the General Assembly were controlled by special interests. The statists[5] just have to wait until they control both houses of the General Assembly and the governorship and then continue their symbiotic relationship with the special interests to sacrifice the interest of the general citizen for the special interests.

---

[5] A *statist* is one who promotes the size and power of the State over the citizen, contrary to the intention of the American Revolution.

Chapter 3

Good Government and Article 1, Section 2 of the Connecticut Constitution

THE DEFINITION OF *good government* referred to by James Madison in the *Federalist Papers* involves two things: "first, fidelity to the object of government, which is the happiness of the people; secondly, a knowledge of the means by which that object can be best attained."[6] This is not the happiness of a special class of citizen, such as a public employee, but rather of the citizen qua citizen. The substance of this sentiment is stated in the Connecticut State Constitution in Article 1, Section 2: "All political power is inherent in the people, and all free governments are founded on their authority, *and instituted for their benefit…*"[7] That means that anything the government does must benefit the general citizen. If the government favors one group of citizens over another group, that action is void as exceeding the powers of our constitution. But the only effective way that Connecticut can free itself from the special interests that control it is by electing an independent governor and enough legislators of any party who are not beholden to the state or the public unions. This sort of governor and legislators could remove

---

[6] *The Federalist Papers* (New York: The New American Library, Inc., 1961), 380.

[7] Emphasis added.

the myriad preferences given to the public unions and special interests to the detriment of the general citizen.

Before I touch on some of these special benefits and how I highlighted them on my campaign, the constitutional logic of Article 1, Section 2 should be read in light of the preceding Article 1, Section 1 that "no man or set of men are entitled to exclusive public emoluments or privileges from the community." You probably had not heard of public emoluments as our statist jurists like the power of the State and go along with it. After all, all the judges in our State get their checks from Hartford. They are members of the court family, specifically, but *the Hartford Club,* generally. *The Hartford Club* is all the people in the State of Connecticut who receive a check from the State or who have a contract to do business with the State. The outside contractors have made their relationships. They have made their contracts. They have made their contacts. They are now on the inside with a steady stream of work. Don't rock the boat. Whether that contract was won through the best competitive bid or whether it included having someone's son, daughter, spouse, relative, friend, or sycophant on a payroll or as a subcontractor, the outside contractor is in. Don't upset the applecart.

It is a no-brainer for the state employee. Don't bite the hand that feeds you. Don't ruin a good thing where not only do you earn more money, benefits, disability, medical care, pension promises, and health insurance than a comparable position in the private sector, but you also have greater job security. It is like two levels of employment between public and private employment. Is that fair to the private-sector workers, who make up the vast majority of workers in the state? Is that fair to the general citizen?

On the campaign trail, I had a series of graphs from the Pew Foundation that had compared the pay and benefits of the public sector throughout the fifty states. I carried one of their graphs around to show where Connecticut fell amongst the fifty states. Connecticut was the best! We won! We were the highest! We were the most! Isn't that great? I knew Connecticut was a great state!

Oh? …Wait?… Paying the most and having generous disability benefits for state employees aren't winning for the private citizen? You mean, a State doesn't want to win that competition? You mean, by overpaying and overcompensating the public sector, we make it harder for regular citizens? You mean, we make it harder for companies to stay in business or to open businesses when the State imposes a bigger burden than neighboring states? You mean, we chase people with money and ideas out of the state? You mean, we depress the price of real estate so that people can't leave the state because their real estate is underwater, where it is worth less than their mortgage and home equity credit line? The homeowner will have to pay money to make up for that difference in order to sell their house to move to a state that didn't win the competition of giving the highest pay and most benefits to state employees and retirees. This is not to disparage the hardworking state employees who are our mothers and fathers, sisters and brothers, sons and daughters, and neighbors and friends. They have a good deal. You would take it too. But how to strike a balance that is fair to the state employees and the general citizenry? That is the question. How to be fair to both?

The Pew research showed that Connecticut was 42 percent above the pay and benefits that a comparable position in the private sector would earn on the national level. My point on the campaign trail was not to focus on the 42 percent. There are assumptions in polls or research, and if you change some of those assumptions, then your numbers shift. It was not a matter of whether it was 42 percent or 35 percent or 28 percent; the point is that Connecticut was the winner out of fifty states and, thereby, the loser! This is not fair to the general citizen. This is not fair to your neighbors and friends, sons and daughters, mothers and fathers, and sisters and brothers who work in the private sector.

Consider further that a public *emolument* is "the returns arising from office or employment usually in the form of compensation or perquisites."[8] While an emolument is pay and benefits for working for the government, Article 1, Section 1 of the Connecticut

---

[8] "Emolument," merriam-webster.com.

Constitution prevents exclusive emolument or privileges from the community to any one man or woman or set of men or women to the exclusion of others. You can't pass a law or, otherwise, legislate to favor your friends or supporters. *Emolument* became a vogue term when those who could not accept the election of President Donald Trump by over sixty million citizens in 2016 looked for ways to undercut or attack his presidency as opposed to working together to address problems in America. Suddenly, the arcane concept of emolument became new again. Articles were published, and letters were written. The U.S. President was likely receiving an emolument. The statists, who love the state and oppose those who would question its size and girth, salivated at finding an emolument. To call excess compensation and benefits paid to public employees and in excess of the private sector an emolument prohibited by Article 1, Section 1 of the Connecticut Constitution, on the other hand, is something a statist and Connecticut judge would run from. Again, Article 1, Section 1 of the Connecticut Constitution commands that "no man or set of men are entitled to exclusive public emoluments or privileges from the community."

The prohibition on emoluments should be kept in mind when reading Article 1, Section 2 of the Connecticut Constitution that all free governments are instituted for the benefit of the citizen. Isn't that why there was a revolution against Great Britain? Was not the American experiment in democracy significant as it would be by the people and for the people and not for a special class of citizen? The authority for the entire government of the state of Connecticut is only for the benefit of the general citizen. There is no authority to benefit a special class of citizen. This should not surprise you. A survey of Connecticut's New England sister state constitutions reveals that each state has similar language—namely, that all free governments are instituted for the benefit of the citizen.

The following are excerpts from the constitutions of the New England sister states:

Government is instituted for the common good; for the protection, safety, prosperity and happiness of the people; **and not for the profit, honor, or private interest of any one man, family, or class of men**: Therefore the people alone have an incontestable, unalienable, and indefeasible right to institute government; and to reform, alter, or totally change the same, when their protection, safety, prosperity and happiness require it. (Massachusetts Constitution, Part the First Article VII; emphasis added)

That government is, or ought to be, instituted for the common benefit, protection, and security of the people, nation, or community, **and not for the particular emolument or advantage of any single person, family, or set of persons, who are a part only of that community;** and that the community hath an indubitable, unalienable, and indefeasible right, to reform or alter government, in such manner as shall be, by that community, judged most conducive to the public weal. (Vermont Constitution, Chapter 1; emphasis added)

Government being instituted for the common benefit, protection, and security, of the whole community, **and not for the private interest or emolument of any one man, family, or class of men**; therefore, whenever the ends of government are perverted, and public liberty manifestly endangered, and all other means of redress are ineffectual, the people may, and of right ought to reform the old, or establish a new government. The doctrine of nonresistance against arbitrary power, and oppression, is absurd, slavish, and destructive of the good and happiness of mankind. (New Hampshire Constitution, Part 1, Article 10; emphasis added)

All power is inherent in the people; all free governments are founded in their authority and **instituted for their benefit**; they have therefore an unalienable and indefeasible right to institute government, and to alter, reform, or totally change the same, when their safety and happiness require it. (Maine Constitution, Article 1, Section 2; emphasis added)

All political power is inherent in the people, and all free governments are founded on their authority, and **instituted for their benefit**; and they have at all times an undeniable and indefeasible right to alter their form of government in such manner as they may think expedient. (Connecticut Constitution, Article 1, Section 2; emphasis added)

All free governments are **instituted for the protection, safety, and happiness of the people.** All laws, therefore, should be made for the good of the whole; and the burdens of the state ought to be fairly distributed among its citizens. No person shall be deprived of life, liberty or property without due process of law, nor shall any person be denied equal protection of the laws. No otherwise qualified person shall, solely by reason of race, gender or handicap be subject to discrimination by the state, its agents or any person or entity doing business with the state.

> Nothing in this section shall be construed to
> grant or secure any right relating to abortion or
> the funding thereof. (Rhode Island Constitution,
> Article 1, Section 2; emphasis added)

Reading the excerpts from the other states of New England underlines the nature of the constitutions of each state—that this revolution of Rule-of-Law governments was for the benefit of the people and nation and not for a special subset of citizens; otherwise, it becomes a prohibited emolument.

If you looked into the other fifty states, I am comfortable that you would find similar language. How could it not be? The statists propose that "all free governments are instituted for the benefit of the insiders." But that is not what it says. But as long as the dead-enders pull the levers of power in Hartford and act like the *Chavistas* in the failed country of Venezuela—where over 80 percent of the citizens are malnourished, and basic medical supplies are not even available, and the Chavistas keep their foot on the throats of their fellow Venezuelans, Connecticut will continue to operate for the benefit of the politically strong, the insiders, to the detriment of the politically weak, the common citizen.

Chapter 4

The "New England" Average

THE OTHER MEANING of Article 1, Section 2 is that there is no authority in the Connecticut Constitution for the governor or the legislature to give the people's money away. That is a pretty obvious statement, but as long as the dead-enders control Hartford and as long as statists people our Supreme Court, the people's money will continue to be given away to the connected and politically powerful. And what is meant by giving away the people's money? It is when one spends more on something than one has to. If a hammer can be bought for ten dollars, one is not authorized to buy the same hammer for fifteen dollars. That would be wasting five dollars of the people's money. What constitution would countenance such an abuse? None. But it goes on as long as one party controls the levers of power and keeps the palms of their allies greased to keep their alliance in power. Doesn't that ring familiar to The Chicago Tragedy, which is lethal to young men of color in jurisdictions where one party has had political control for decades?[9]

---

[9] The Chicago tragedy is where, prior to 2016, an average of two young men of color were dying a violent death in Chicago every day, and yet the media elite like the *New York Times,* the *Washington Post,* the *Los Angeles Times, CNN, MSNBC, NBC News, CBS, ABC, VOX, HuffPost,* the *New Yorker, Bloomberg News,* and the nation were silent to this tragedy. And we continue to be silent in the aftermath of the killing of George Floyd in Minneapolis, Minnesota, on May 25, 2020. The Chicago tragedy encompasses the loss of life not just in Chicago, but also in cities like Baltimore, Philadelphia, St. Louis, and Detroit,

So it is settled that the government cannot give the people's money away.

So what would giving money away look like? If you pay 5 percent or more than the going rate, you are giving away the peoples' money. The State of Connecticut has an annual budget of over twenty billion dollars. If they give away 5 percent in one year, then that would be over one billion dollars. One billion is one hundred million dollars ten times. What could one do with one million dollars? Multiply that by one thousand. That is a lot of money. While I appreciate there is no exact measurement of what something should cost, and sometimes you have to outbid the next guy to hire an employee or convince a contractor to work for the state, 3 percent is adequate and certainly enforceable as a margin of error. Beyond 3 percent and the State is not being prudent with the people's money. If Pew Research says that Connecticut is paying salaries and giving benefits that exceed the national private sector by 42 percent, that would be criminal, but the statist Connecticut Supreme Court would never raise a hand to stop such an abuse of the Connecticut citizenry. Those contractual terms to employees and private contractors in excess of 3 percent over the going rate is a synopsis of why Connecticut is in financial distress and emblematic of the state's control over the citizen.

Arguments are made that things are more expensive in Connecticut than in other areas of the country, and for that reason, our kind and well-meaning state employees should be paid more. To that I say that there is the hybrid category of the "New England Average." That means, if one took the pay and benefits that the six New England states pay for a certain position and the benefits that go with it, that would be the *New England average*. This compensates for the argument that things are more expensive in New England than they are in Alabama, Mississippi, or North Dakota.

---

to name the more significant cities. Why are these boys' and men's lives not worthy of attention? Senator Cory Booker chided the nation in the past that "silence is complicity." Are we all complicit in the Chicago tragedy despite the many who scale their soapboxes to say how wonderful they are as human beings in their self-flagellation in the aftermath of the killing of George Floyd?

And while there is a difference in the cost of living between Vermont and Massachusetts, each state has some things that are more expensive, and each state has some things that are less expensive. Housing in Vermont may be cheaper than down South, but products may be more expensive as things need to be shipped greater distances to serve fewer people. Vermont only has about six hundred thousand people. Connecticut has about 3.5 million people in a more compact space. This can make goods or services less expensive in Connecticut.

If we look at where the six states ended up on the Pew Research with Connecticut at 42 percent above the private sector, Massachusetts at 19 percent above the private sector, Rhode Island at 24 percent above the private sector, Maine at 8 percent above the private sector, New Hampshire at 10 percent above the private sector, and Vermont at 2 percent above the private sector, that totals 105, which you divide by six and come up with the New England average of 17.5 percent above the national private sector. Connecticut is 20 percent higher than that!

If you took the bloated costs of Connecticut out of the calculation and based Connecticut on what the other five New England states pay, the New England Average would be 12.6 percent above the national private sector instead of 42 percent higher, like Connecticut. Both measures clearly exceed what our constitution authorizes! If Connecticut goes 5 percent above the New England Average, then we exceed our constitutional limit. Using the New England Average of 12.6 percent, which does not include Connecticut's bloated numbers, Connecticut is 29.4 percent higher, an unconstitutional occurrence. You might have a similar circumstance in your state? Or your state is run more for the benefit of the ordinary citizen rather than for a special class of citizen that has captured a state.

Chapter 5

Accountability of the State to the Citizen

On May 25, 2020, forty-six-year-old George Floyd, a black man, died in Minneapolis, Minnesota, while police officer Derek Chauvin, a white officer, knelt on Mr. Floyd's neck for over eight minutes despite the plea by Mr. Floyd that he could not breathe. The arrest was for allegedly passing a counterfeit twenty-dollar bill. Messrs. Floyd and Chauvin knew each other as they both worked at the same El Nuevo Rodeo club in Minneapolis.[10] According to the article, Officer Chauvin had worked security on the outside of the club, and Mr. Floyd had worked security on the inside of the club. The death, which was recorded on video, set off months of protesting in the United States, some peaceful and some not peaceful with vandalism, looting, and burned buildings. Protests also erupted worldwide against police brutality. Some third parties took advantage of the legitimate peaceful protests to "distract and destruct."[11] These third-party agitators were not interested in the

---

[10] Minyvonne Burke and Jaime Longoria, "George Floyd and Officer Who Knelt on His Neck Had Worked at Same Nightclub, Former Owner Says," May 29, 2020, https://www.nbcnews.com/news/us-news/george-floyd-officer-who-kneeled-his-neck-had-worked-same-n1217976.

[11] President Derrick Johnson of the National Association for the Advancement of Colored People observed after the tragedy that one should be cognizant of the

legitimate message of the protestors, but preferred to distract from that message and destruct what was around them. Why did these buildings burn? It did not and does not advance the issues that the peaceful protestors were promoting when the businesses of minority as well as non-minority business owners are destroyed. It destroys wealth precisely in challenged communities. It eliminates jobs for just those people living in the challenged communities. It eliminates goods and services that are provided in the challenged communities. It can take decades to build a business up, one day at a time. It can take "anti-fascists" and anarchists minutes to destroy that business, the jobs it provides, the goods and services it provides, and the tax income beneficial to the community—all in minutes. People speak of food deserts, where there is a lack of fresh, quality produce and food options in poorer neighborhoods. When businesses large and small come in to provide a better selection of food, that is a social good. Yet these protestors gleefully enter and destroy all that and negatively impact the lives of the people in these communities that they are ostensibly there to help! "Take your mask and helmet off and show your face."

The outrage and demonstrations following the death of George Floyd were primarily focused on police brutality and accountability for actions by the police. There were headline grabbers to say that Officer Chauvin and others had been fired. In other jurisdictions like Atlanta, Georgia, other headlines claimed that an officer had been fired. As a general matter, you cannot fire a police officer, just as you cannot fire a bad public-school teacher or civil servant where there is a public union and collective bargaining. Yes, at some point the administrators can terminate a public worker, and maybe it sticks. That is to quibble. *Firing* is not the right word. Collective-bargaining agreements set up a whole host of protections for their union members versus their public employers. There are naturally union-paid advocates and even union attorneys to go to battle to keep the union

---

threats of the COVID-19 that was disproportionately claiming black lives and that some people show up at peaceful demonstrations with their own motives.

member in his or her job, regardless of how horrendous the employee may have been—the commonweal be damned.

A public union is bound by the law of fiduciary duty to promote and protect public employees first, the union second, and then whatever job they are supposed to be doing third. So if it is teaching children in a public school, the children's welfare and benefit come third after the union member and the union. A union is an organic being and is obligated to live and prosper. That living and prospering only occur with a stable or growing union membership as well as a steady supply of union dues. If there are no union members, then there are no dues and no union. This is not to slight or impugn our friends and neighbors, brothers and sisters, fathers and mothers, and sons and daughters who work diligently and sometimes heroically as teachers, peace officers, firefighters, public-works employees, building inspectors, health inspectors, crossing guards, public-refuse workers, sanitation employees, registrars, tax collectors and tax assessors, laboratory technicians, first selectmen, mayors, representative-town committee members, planning-and-zoning board members, zoning enforcement officers, public-works engineers, dockmasters, beach attendants, lifeguards, nurses, health aides, truck drivers, town clerks, etc. They are the lifeblood of making our local, state, and federal governments work! The power of the public unions, however, has gone too far in protecting problematic employees.

Effectively, a public employee cannot be fired. Perhaps, they are placed on administrative leave with pay. If the union and attorney for the public employee challenge the firing first through administrative channels as there needs to be a paper record of warnings and bad annual reviews in the file, it is an expensive long process. There need to be chances given at improving and getting one's job back. If the administrative process doesn't work out in the employee's favor, then the union and/or employee can sue the local, state, or federal government in civil court to challenge that decision. There are repeated stories of a judge deciding either at the trial level or at a further appellate level that the employee should not have been fired for such and such a reason and that the employee must be given his or her job back, plus back pay, vacation time, sick days, retirement days, personal days, disability eligibility, pension credits, etc. When faced with this prospect, a town, state, or federal administrator may opt for reassignment or, in the alternative, the ultimate unconstitutional concept: the rubber room.

What is a rubber room? This is, traditionally, where incompetent teachers are put to show up for work, but not do any work. They sit in the room all day, read the paper, do crossword puzzles, chat with others in the rubber room, call friends and family, maybe look for other work in the same school system, etc. This is seen as cheaper than running through the whole administrative process that public unions and collective bargaining have established to put the public employee above accountability to the citizen. A rubber room, by its very definition, is violently unconstitutional. At no point in drafting, debating, and enacting Connecticut's constitution was it contemplated that one could waste the people's money on incompetents in the service of the people. The people's money cannot be wasted on people who are better suited to other types of work in the private sector. Everybody has things that they can do well. Everybody has skills and something to offer. "All free governments are instituted for the benefit of the citizen." This is for the general citizen and not a special class of citizen. Rubber rooms and public employees who are extremely difficult to terminate are unconstitutional. The people's money cannot be wasted. It's in our constitution. But, alas, Connecticut is not run for the general citizen, but rather, it is run by and for the public employees and other special interests.

Another canard that has been repeated after the tragedy of the killing of George Floyd[12] is the need to increase funding of educa-

---

[12] By referencing the death of George Floyd, this is not to say that the killing of other citizens such as Breonna Taylor is not of the same weight. The killing of Breonna Taylor, in some sense, is more alarming as it occurred in her own home. According to reports, Louisville, Kentucky, police executed a no-knock warranted search of Ms. Taylor's apartment late at night to search for illegal drugs. Ms. Taylor, an EMT worker, and her boyfriend were allegedly in the bedroom when the police officers entered her apartment. According to a civil suit filed on behalf of Ms. Taylor's estate, the officers did not identify themselves and shot

tion. That is always a meritorious endeavor as our children are our future. But one must pay attention to what the statists[13] are proposing. They are mostly proposing that there be more public-union jobs created that pay more dues to public unions so that the public unions can get their politicians elected so that these very same politicians can deliver benefits and job security to the union members above and beyond those available in the private sector. Can one ask these statists whether improved education includes school choice of more public-charter schools and vouchers for nonpublic schools, such as Catholic schools for poor urban and rural students, and what is their answer? The answer is, invariably, no. The reason is that public-charter schools are not customarily staffed by public unions, though not always, and that means that more of our children would be taught outside of the public-school monopoly of the public unions like the National Education Association and the American Federation of Teachers. That would mean fewer union dues flowing to the state and national headquarters of these unions and their bosses. That would run contrary to their legal fiduciary duty to their members and themselves to expand public unions. Students will forever remain third on their priority list.

Around 2017 there were about nine thousand two hundred students in Connecticut's twenty-four public-charter schools. This is less than 2 percent of the students enrolled in K-12 schools in Connecticut. Nonetheless, around seven thousand young black and Hispanic students were on wait lists to get into these charter schools, which the statists prevent from expanding to favor the state's unions over the black and Hispanic students whose parents and guardians would like greater educational choice. The largest teacher's union, the NEA, is practically giddy in their efforts to prevent the expansion

---

Ms. Taylor whilst Mr. Kenneth Walker, a licensed gun owner, shot back, thinking that someone was breaking in. The police state that they did identify themselves. (Christopher Brito, "Family Sues after 26-year-old EMT Is Shot and Killed by Police in Her Own Home," May 15, 2020, https://www.cbsnews.com/news/breonna-taylor-family-sues-wrongful-death-killed-police-louisville/.)

[13] A *statist* is one who promotes the expansion, power, and control of the State over the citizen.

of charter schools to serve primarily black, Hispanic, and Asian students on a national level, boasting a newspaper headline on its home page, "Strikes, Pay Rises and Charter Protests: America's Exhausting Exhilarating Year" (nea.org). So the NEA finds protesting against charters exhilarating? How sad.

It is respectfully submitted that the demand for accountability for policing should also apply to our school systems. The difficulty of inquiring of and firing problematic police officers who may impugn the reputation of the rest of their brethren is similar to the difficulty of inquiring of and firing problematic teachers who are otherwise relegated to rubber rooms or reassigned within the school system and is unconstitutional. Our governments were formed on these shores for the general citizen. But the general citizen is blocked from having a government accountable to the general citizen by public union collective bargaining.

Brought into the light of day, the concept of collective bargaining by public unions is anathema to our Connecticut Constitution and accountability. Public unions will find that the justification for collective, bargaining, binding-arbitration "jumped the shark"[14] with the killing of George Floyd and the subsequent demands for accountability for police officers. Public union collective-bargaining agreements prevent effective accountability for the acts and omissions of police officers, teachers, and other public workers to the citizens they are sworn to serve. In Connecticut, they have resulted in the highest pay, benefits, disability, personal days, sick days, pensions, and health

---

[14] "Jump the shark" came from a TV program called *Happy Days* in the 1970s. A central character, the Fonz, was so cool in everything he did. He was so cool he could get the jukebox to play music for free (that is a machine that you put money into at a restaurant or diner, and then you can select one or more songs for the jukebox to play.) just by giving it a gentle hip check. Only the Fonz could pull that off. The series was hugely popular, but apparently, when the family that he rented from went to Los Angeles, he went with them for vacation. At the beach he got into a competition with a cool local guy, and they competed by water-ski jumping over a caged shark. The show spiraled after that episode. "Jump the shark" now indicates the point in time at which a show goes south.

care outstripping all other states and far exceeding the New England Average of compensation and benefits of public employees.

Alas, it does not stop there as public unions have negotiated contractual terms that supersede the laws of the state. That is correct. There are laws in the *Connecticut General Statutes* that will not be applied to public unions. This highlights their preferred status and is commensurate with their political control over the state enabled by statist politicians who promote the state over the citizen. "State employee contract provisions may supersede contrary provisions of state laws or regulations that relate to state employee wages, hours, and conditions of employment."[15] The legislature and governor may have carefully crafted statutory laws to address issues in the state. But these duly passed laws matter not if in negotiations over the employment terms for state employees or after a collective-bargaining decision, terms contrary to state law are adopted. That is supersedence. "Among laws that have been superseded by contracts are laws governing payments into the pension system, employee overtime, complaints against the police, Freedom of Information and the grievance process." "Professors at a public university sexually harassed students for years before their behavior was revealed."[16] Nurses who were fired for abusing mentally ill patients at a public hospital were rehired, only to be arrested again for abusing patients."[17] "A police officer who on camera used profanity, threatened violence, and told an immigrant to leave the country was fired and then re-hired after the union took the city to court."[18]

How about a state law that says an employee can only be on paid administrative leave for fourteen days, and a state worker took

---

[15] Suzanne Bates, "Supersedence: The Consequences of Government Unions' Special Privileges," *Yankee Institute Policy Paper*, series 2019, vol. 4.

[16] Id., citing Chris Powell, "State E=Employee Contracts Can Nullify State Law," *Journal Inquirer*, April 18, 2018.

[17] "Supersedence," citing Marc Fitch, "The Fitch Files: Whiting Hospital Was Forced to Rehire Employees Terminated for Abuse," *Yankee Institute,* March 28, 2018.

[18] "Supersedence," citing Associated Press, "City Ordered to Rehire Cop Fired for Berating Immigrant," April 11, 2018.

unlimited paid administrative leave during an investigation for sixty-nine weeks. That is well beyond a paid administrative year when you are only supposed to get two weeks. And Connecticut is run by whom for whom?

Under the State Employees Bargaining Agent Coalition (SEBAC) Agreement from 2017, state employees were scheduled to receive a 3.5 percent wage increase on July 1, 2020. This is months after the crippling coronavirus lockdown that occurred from the spread of the COVID-19/novel coronavirus that emanated from China since late 2019. With stay-at-home orders and social distancing, Connecticut's economy, like much of the nation, had suffered grievously as had individuals with loss of jobs, loss of hours, and loss of businesses that had taken decades to build. Breitbart has estimated that over one hundred thousand people in a state with about 3.5 million people had lost their jobs. The sales tax and income tax receipts for the State of Connecticut were projected to decline 11 percent in 2020. Where would the State look to cover the budgetary shortfalls? How many state employees would have to be furloughed or laid off? What adjustments would have to be made to have sufficient funds to continue running the state government? The statists that run Connecticut did not announce any furloughs or pending layoffs. Instead, Governor Lamont proceeded with three hundred and fifty million dollars in raises for public-union workers in these historically and economically challenging times. That is a disconnect between running the government for the happiness of the citizen and for the benefit of the citizen, the general citizen, as opposed to those who run the state for their own benefit. "Public sector compensation has overwhelmed the state budget and economy."[19]

How is that right? In 2019 Andrew Biggs of the American Enterprise Institute had determined that in 2017, "Connecticut public sector workers enjoyed a 51 percent compensation premium over

---

[19] Dr. Susan Berry, "Connecticut State Workers to Receive $350 Million in Raises as 100,000 Lose Private Sector Jobs," April 21, 2020, https://www.breitbart.com/politics/2020/04/21/connecticut-state-workers-to-receive-350-million-in-raises-as-100000-lose-private-sector-jobs/, quoting....

the state's private sector workers."[20] And during the worst recession since the Great Depression of the 1930s, the state public employees received a 3.5 percent raise. For whom is the State of Connecticut being run?

---

[20] Id.

Chapter 6

Reform of SEBAC and
Other State Contracts

S o how else might constitutional principles be applied to Connecticut to save the state? There was an issue during the gubernatorial campaign in 2017–2018 that captured the imagination for a while. That was the SEBAC Agreement, or the 2017 State Employees Bargaining Agent Coalition Agreement.

On July 31, 2017, Lieutenant Governor Nancy Wyman cast the tie-breaking vote on a state employee labor concession package. This new contract was projected to save 1.5 billion dollars over a two-year budget period and covered more than thirty public unions, which represent our kind and well-meaning state workers. With this saving came a four-year period of no layoffs and an extension of existing union contracts until 2027. That sounds like a long time to the layman as well as to attorneys.

Senator Martin Looney, the top Democrat in the Senate, was quoted as saying, "We're going to respect our workers and their right to collectively bargain, and this is a reasonable negotiation and reasonable result both for the state and its unionized workers."

The actual standard of whether something qualifies as good government, however, was put forward by James Madison in "Federalist No. 62": "A good government implies two things: first, fidelity to the object of government, which is the happiness of the people: secondly, a knowledge of the means by which that object can be best attained."[21]

A ten-year irrevocable contract is not good government.

We have our state constitution to "define, secure, and perpetuate the liberties, rights and privileges which [the people] have derived from their ancestors…"[22] "That the great and essential principles of liberty and free government may be recognized and established."[23]

Putting a four-year fence around the public unions of no layoffs and increases in pay plus locking in the employment terms for ten years until 2027 favors the Hartford Club. It does not advance the happiness of the people. Could that have been a bridge too far? If ten years is okay, why not lock the terms in for twenty years? Did the proponents maintain that they had created a superstate within the state? If all state government employment expenses, wages, benefits, health care, and disability amounted to 40 percent of the biannual budget, does that mean that this superstate has been cordoned off and cannot be touched for ten years?

How does this square with our constitution? First we come to Article 1, Section 1 where "no set of men [or women] are entitled to exclusive public emoluments or privileges from the community" (profit arising from office, employment, or labor). Is a ten-year agreement a public emolument?

Our government is divided into the legislative, executive, and judicial branches.[24]

Our government can pass a law by a simple majority vote of the house of the General Assembly and then the Senate followed by the governor's signature.[25] This implies that the same law could be overturned or amended the following year by a simple majority. If the governor does not sign what the legislature has passed, the General Assembly house and the Senate can override that veto by two-thirds

---

[21] *The Federalist Papers*, p. 380.
[22] Preamble to the Connecticut Constitution.
[23] Article 1, Connecticut Constitution.
[24] Article 2, Connecticut Constitution.
[25] Article 4, Section 15, Connecticut Constitution.

majority.[26] And in the same fashion a law can be undone the following year.

Our constitution can be amended by three-quarters vote of the General Assembly House and Senate, which would then submit the issue to a majority referendum of the citizens.[27]

The General Assembly may even call for a constitutional convention by two-thirds vote of each house, provided one has not occurred in the previous ten years.[28]

So there are numerous ways to pass laws and amend them annually, and there are even ways to amend our constitution from time to time, but we were led to believe that the labor agreement passed at the end of July 2017 could not be amended or altered for ten years? Does this not appear to be a superstate within the state? How can our constitution provide for a method by which our laws can be changed and our constitution can be amended, but the labor agreement from that summer is inviolate for ten years? You do not have to be an attorney to ask whether this is a bridge too far.

It is, in fact, *ultra vires* and void *ab initio*. The legislature and governor can vest no more power into their actions than that granted by our state constitution. You may recall some lessons from your middle-school civics lessons. We instituted a limited government for the people and by the people. The government can only do what we have authorized it to do. All powers not granted to the government are retained by the people. Therefore, if a state union contract is approved by a simple majority of the legislature and signed by the governor, it follows that that same contract can be voided by a simple majority of the legislature and signature of the governor one month later. The ink in the governor's pen does not have some extra strength to put such a contract out of reach of reversal by the same steps as it was enacted. While it is reasonable for the legislature to make a contract for one bridge or one road, which is enforceable, you cannot take 35 percent of the budget and put it off-limits for the legislature

---

[26] Article 4, Section 15, Connecticut Constitution.

[27] Article 12, Connecticut Constitution.

[28] Article 13, Connecticut Constitution.

and governor for four, ten, or twenty years. If 35 percent is okay, why not 65 percent? It is a bridge too far. You cannot disenfranchise subsequent voters or legislators. It is like telling a citizen who was seventeen then that their vote will have no impact on 35–40 percent of the state budget until they are twenty-seven years old. That is patently false.

Yet what can the citizens of Connecticut do? The statist Supreme Court will uphold whatever their fellow statists will tell them to uphold. Yet that is an incorrect result. A statist is one who values the state over the citizen.

Think about a person's life when they have entered into a contract with another party. Maybe when they opened a bank account, they had to sign or agree to various terms. When buying an iPhone, there may be things that one agrees to in order to download something or have access to a particular application. I don't read those disclosures either. One just clicks it and moves on. In the movie *Jexi*, the main character agrees to the terms of agreement, only to learn that he has handed over all his information to the virtual assistant with significant consequences. When you buy an automobile or lease an automobile, you will sign paperwork. Some of that paperwork is required by the State, but other parts are to protect the seller of the car. Maybe you have signed a lease to rent a house or apartment, or you signed a contract to buy a condominium or a house. If the parties to a contract come to a disagreement that they cannot resolve, sometimes they might sue each other, and to do that you go to an attorney, who brings an action in a court. If you are renting an apartment in Connecticut, then the attorney is not going to file that action in Arizona as Arizona has nothing to do with an apartment rental in Connecticut. In fact, it is possible that neither the landlord nor the tenant has ever been to Arizona, in which case Arizona would not even have personal jurisdiction over either person to judge the case. The dispute doesn't even involve Arizona as the apartment, landlord, and tenant are all in Connecticut. So it would correctly be filed and processed in Connecticut. And what law would be applied? The law of Connecticut. Sometimes the disclosures that one agrees to state in them that any dispute will be first brought to arbitration in *X* state and *X* arbitration panel and that the laws of *X* state will govern the agreement. Let's say that Google is located in California, and the customer is located in North Carolina. The Google agreement will probably say that their agreement is governed by the laws of California, where they have their headquarters. That makes sense as at least one party has a connection to that state and its laws.

So for the landlord-tenant dispute in Connecticut, the law of Connecticut would apply. And what is the law of the State of Connecticut? It is comprised of many things. Preliminarily, it involves statutory law in statutes that govern the relationship between landlord and tenant. Then there are individual cases that arose before the case at hand that may have interpreted or applied the state statutes to particular legal disputes. These are called "common law" precedents, and findings of law are sometimes contained in these cases. That is also law. So the law that is applied to the dispute is attached to the contract or lease that is involved. And what is the ultimate law of the state? It is the constitution. That means a copy of our constitution is attached to every contract entered into in the State of Connecticut that will apply Connecticut law. It does not matter whether that contract was entered into this year or whether it was entered into nine years ago; the Connecticut Constitution is attached to all Connecticut contracts. And our Connecticut Constitution is attached to the SEBAC Agreement and all previous agreements between the State and public unions. And our constitution is attached to all legislation that is passed by the General Assembly and signed by the governor. And our constitution says in Article 1, Section 2 that you cannot give the people's money away. The state constitutions of all fifty states should have something similar in it. And since giving the people's money away is unenforceable, the question is not *whether* the wages, benefits, disability, and pension benefits of Connecticut state employees and retirees can be adjusted to the New England Average, but *when*.

Since the Connecticut Constitution is attached to the SEBAC Agreement, it can be reopened as violative of the constitution to the extent it is unfair to the general citizenry by favoring the politically connected as elements of prohibited emoluments are contained therein. But this will not and cannot happen until Connecticut regains its free will. And if your State is controlled by self-serving special interests, your State will not be able to do anything to save itself until your State has regained its free will to act for the benefit of the general citizenry and sets wages, benefits, and disability benefits that approach those available in the free market and surrounding states. That is only fair to those who do not work for the State. I recognize, as a mere fact of political power, that the public sector will earn more in pay and benefits than the private sector due to political muscle, but how big should that inequality be? How big an inequality should the citizens of Connecticut accept? Is there an inequality in your state? The first step to fairness to the citizens of Connecticut is to adhere to the Connecticut Constitution. And that requires the pay and benefits to get to the New England average.

This is not just a duty to correct this unfairness to the general citizen, but it is also an obligation to our children, retirees, and public workers. What can we afford for present and future state employees? Who will be left to carry the burden of past promises to future state retirees? You need to have people in the state in order to make the budgets work. An exaggerated case is that if there are no people left who are working in the private sector, then existing state workers cannot be paid, nor can health care or pension promises be met for past state workers. How can we make Connecticut more competitive as a place to do business, a place where we want to stay and prosper, a place where people want to raise their families, and a place where retirees want to enjoy their golden years with friends and family?

In the recent past the Democrat Senator Bob Duff, Senator Martin Looney, and house member Joe Aresimowicz could be likened to the Three Horsemen. They have been repeatedly reelected and effectively have run Connecticut for years as General Assembly leaders of the Democrat majority in the House and Senate. They have promoted themselves, in my opinion, as friends of public unions. On the one hand, they have delivered plenty for public-union workers in the state; hence, the 51 percent premium earned over the private sector if you lay credence to the American Enterprise Institute study or 42 percent higher than the national private sector if you give credence to the Pew Research data. It is not whether it is 51 percent or 42 percent as at the end of the day, the Three Horsemen have delivered pay and benefits that far outstrip the private sector, a constitutional imbalance. As in a pyramid scheme, the first group of investors get a nice payoff above their private-sector neighbors, but then the rest of the investors will see the promises evaporate. If there are no jobs in the state, then no taxes are paid, and there is nothing to distribute to future state retirees. There are no health-care benefits. This would suggest that the Three Horsemen will not deliver on their lofty promises—bromides and riches. Are they really friends of labor when Connecticut cannot and will not be able to afford all these benefits above the New England Average?

A quick review of numbers, which is not my forte, will exhibit the problem. Connecticut has about a twenty-billion-dollar annual budget. About 30 percent of that budget goes to debt service for money borrowed and pension and retirement benefits for people who no longer work for the state. That leaves one with 70 percent of twenty billion dollars, which would be fourteen billion dollars. Estimates of Connecticut's pension, health care, and debt obligations range from sixty-two to sixty-seven billion dollars or more. Last year, the General Assembly kicked the can further down the road and pushed off collections to try to meet future pension and debt obligations decades hence, to increase the total cost by billions, but to make today's budget "balanced" so that the Three Horsemen and their statist allies can be reelected.

How can a fourteen-billion-dollar budget, before the economy was hammered by the coronavirus lockdown of 2020, ever hope to chip away at over sixty-seven billion dollars in debt? Do the statists propose that an additional three billion dollars can be found somewhere while pension and health-care costs eat up even more of the state budget?

With friends like the Three Horsemen, the outsized promises will not be paid one hundred cents on the dollar. Our state constitution is not a suicide pact. The State has the sovereign power to readjust its obligations and contracts to ensure the survival of the state so that schools, roads, pensions, parks, police, fire and environmental protection, among others, will be provided in the future to the citizens of the state. Our constitution states clearly that the citizens "have at all times an undeniable and indefeasible right to alter their form of government in such manner as they may think expedient."[29] This constitutional language is attached to the SEBAC Agreement.

So once the citizens of the state demand that they be treated fairly and the compensation, benefits, and retirement terms for public-sector workers are closer to the private sector, then there will be a governor and legislature dedicated to fairness.

Even if Connecticut were to regain its free will, there is a fly in the ointment: our Connecticut Supreme Court. Without naming names, it is comprised mostly of statists who have forgotten that they are to favor the citizen over the State. It could be that they went to a law school that taught progressive law, that all should bow before the mighty State. Then there is the problem that the Connecticut Supreme Court and her clerks are members of the Hartford Club. They receive their paychecks from the state government. When the governor and General Assembly demand that the playing field be leveled and that the people's money not be wasted, the Supreme Court, under its present makeup of statists and pro-state sentiments, will back the State and deem the corrective actions of the governor and General Assembly a breach of contract. They might opine that it is well and good to try to balance the state budget and to not hound people and businesses out of the state, but the State entered into a contract with these kind and well-meaning state employees and that, therefore, no changes are allowed to past agreements. The State can only change things going forward. The 2017 SEBAC Agreement claims to last until 2027, so the Connecticut Supreme Court would probably opine that it remain inviolate to honor their allegiance to the power of the State over the citizen. The disenfranchisement of future voters to address 35–40 percent of the state budget will be

---

[29] Article 1, Section 2, Connecticut Constitution.

held to be off the table due to contract law. The statist Supreme Court may allow some minor changes on the edges, but that is it.

The Connecticut Supreme Court would probably overlook the fact that the State of Connecticut is a sovereign state. It cannot go into bankruptcy like a city can; otherwise, a bankruptcy judge would be the governor, General Assembly, and Supreme Court all wrapped into one person. That would be the equivalent of a king or queen. Or how would the politically correct call it: a "kueen"? We don't operate under one-person rule anymore. There was a revolution in the 1770s that you may have heard about. The State of Connecticut may correct its fiscal house at any time under our constitution. The federal courts must follow our interpretation of Connecticut contracts since the Connecticut Supreme Court is the ultimate arbiter of Connecticut contract law, with the proviso that the General Assembly and governor can make changes to contract law by legislation, which the Connecticut Supreme Court then enforces. That Article 1, Section 2 is in the constitution makes Article 1, Section 2 stronger than any previous precedent of the Connecticut State Supreme Court. All previous Connecticut Supreme Court cases are merely persuasive opinions. In other words, all previous decisions are merely recommendations on how the Supreme Court should rule whereas the constitution requires the Supreme Court to follow it. The citation of previous cases decided by a statist court cannot counter the plain meaning of Connecticut's constitution. The highest authority is the written document, our constitution.

The economic havoc wreaked by the COVID-19 pandemic in 2020 thereafter decimated the budgets of cities and states nationwide. The stay-at-home orders contracted economic activity across the nation. Unemployment skyrocketed past thirty million people. A law of economics is that unemployed people generally pay less taxes than employed people. With restaurants, barbers, hairdressers, repair shops, machine shops, and retail shops closed, economic activity contracted. With fewer miles being driven, gas tax receipts declined. With fewer sales taxes, gas taxes, and withholding taxes from wages as well as self-employment taxes from entrepreneurs, the financial condition of towns, cities, and states weakened. Connecticut already had among the top five worst fiscal conditions of the fifty states prior to the COVID-19 pandemic. According to Bloomberg News, the Connecticut legislature's Office of Fiscal Analysis estimated that Connecticut's revenue would plummet by almost 3.2 billion dollars in the fourteen months following the outbreak of the pandemic as income and sales taxes evaporated because of the coronavirus shutdown.[30] The statists have ridden Connecticut so hard since the great recession of 2008–2009 by piling on even more taxes and charges that the state never fully recovered from it unlike most of the other fifty states: "The state never fully recouped all the jobs lost from the Great Recession and Connecticut's economy hasn't grown in the last decade. Fixed costs for debt, health care and employee pensions eat up more than 30% of state spending."[31] That is correct. Around 30 percent of the state's budget doesn't even provide benefits to state residents other than retired state workers. So when Connecticut estimated general-fund declines of 11 percent for fiscal 2021 and 11.8 percent in fiscal 2022, what could be done to save Connecticut? The statists are likely to pile more taxes and fees onto the shrinking private sector. For the statists in Hartford, who like their ideological *Chavista* brethren in Caracas, Venezuela, who have pauperized the citizens of the formerly highest-flying economy in South America, Venezuela, with the largest proven oil reserves in the world, the Hartford *Chavistas* will push for more fees, taxes, and revenues from the citizens and businesses of Connecticut, further ensuring her decline. The fixed costs in the Connecticut state budget are just too high and rising. The Hartford *Chavistas*, as the skilled politicians that they are, will claim to be working for the citizens of Connecticut while they further bury the state. The job losses were so bad that the pandemic erased a full decade of job gains across the nation.[32] With

---

[30] Martin Z. Braun, "Connecticut's $3 Billion Budget Reserve May Be Gone in 14 Months," May 1, 2020.

[31] Id.

[32] Sarah Chaney and Eric Morath, "Decade of Job Gains Erased in April," *Wall Street Journal,* May 9–10, 2020, p. A1.

national job losses in April 2020 as the worst since records have been kept since 1939 for the entire United States, what are the prospects for Connecticut, which had been an economic laggard for the years since the Great Recession?

All is not lost, however. There is hope for Connecticut if she can return to the principles set forth in the state's constitution! "[N]o man or set of men are entitled to…privileges from the community."[33] Being compensated and benefited more than a similar private-sector job is a privilege. "[A]ll free governments are founded on [the people's] authority, and instituted for their benefit."[34] "No hereditary emoluments, privileges or honors, shall ever by granted or conferred in this state."[35]

However, even if the legislators and governor in Hartford were to change course and represent all the citizens of the State of Connecticut versus a privileged category of citizens, the statist judges are likely to continue subjugating the citizen to the power of the State.

---

[33] Article 1, Section 1, Connecticut Constitution.
[34] Article 1, Section 2, Connecticut Constitution.
[35] Article 1, Section 18, Connecticut Constitution.

Chapter 7

Connecticut Court Enforces Nonexistent Rule and Supreme Court Misses Due Process

So how bad is the Connecticut Supreme Court? Read on and you shall see.

I had lived in the town of Greenwich for most of my youth and adult life. Back in 1985, a newly minted attorney, brought an action against the town of Greenwich, challenging a town ordinance that didn't allow nonresidents to go to some town parks and beaches. The one he was most concerned with was Tod's Point, which is over one hundred acres on Long Island Sound that the town had purchased in 1945. At first the old mansion on the property was used to house World War II veterans and their families after World War II. After years of neglect by the town, the town tore that mansion down, but today many of the foundations remain and provide stellar views of Long Island Sound and Long Island beyond. Tod's Point also has wonderful walking trails and a wide, gently sloping, flat beach plus concession stands. And who doesn't like hot dogs, greasy burgers, french fries, and sugary sodas under a hot summer sun at the beach? There is a gatehouse at the entrance to check for beach passes. Apparently, as a law student, this Stamford resident had been part of a successful legal effort to get some parks in New Jersey opened up to the public under a public-trust doctrine. Hats off for good legal work. Urban lore was that this attorney was living at his parents' house in neighboring Stamford at the time that he was denied entrance into this marvelous park, but I don't know that, and he may have owned or rented in Stamford at the time. I know nothing about the rental terms that this Stamford attorney had. Sometimes when one lives at home after college, there are favorable rental rates that include kitchen privileges, occasional prepared meals, decent laundry facilities, a stocked refrigerator, and sometimes even a motor vehicle. This is what I did after graduating from law school. I lived on the third floor and took the train to my job in New York City until I found a decent rental situation on the Upper West Side. It helps you save money too, which is a good thing.

This Stamford attorney was not the first to contest the town's beach admission policy or to question its legality. He was, however, the most successful. When I read about the action, what came to mind was the *Free Lunch Society*. In addition to having my law practice in Old Greenwich since 1989, I had started building houses in New York and then later in Connecticut in 1995. I had also been exposed to economics classes in college, where you learn about supply and demand. In law school we learned that when you are buyer of a property, you can get specific performance of a contract even if your seller doesn't want to sell you his or her house after signing. The reason that you can make the seller sell you their house after you both sign a contract is that every house is unique. No two houses are alike, even in a tract subdivision where the same house plan with the same finishes was selected. There are always differences, like the view, sun exposure, proximity to school, and transportation. Therefore, each house is unique. The factors that go into selecting a house are as long as there are lists of materials. And the market—that is, you and me—takes all the elements of a house into consideration, including its taxation rate and school district, when determining what we would pay for a house. Each buyer—and for that matter, renter—has different objectives and budgets. Some people are just starting families and might put a greater emphasis on the quality and distance to school. Some people might be retiring and not need a big house or care much for the school system. Greenwich was considered then and is still considered today to be a desirable town for its school systems, architecture, neighborhoods, and lower taxes. Stamford is also desirable for its country homes, waterfront neighborhoods, schools, and urban scene. It has it all and has been a great success story compared to what it was in 1963 when we arrived in Stamford to our first rental. Then it consisted of many shuttered manufacturing buildings. Before Connecticut shot itself in the foot when it enacted the ruinous state income tax, Stamford and Fairfield County boasted headquarters of countless Fortune 500 companies. But now that the state has an income tax and one-party rule, businesses have left and continue to leave, and the state consistently underperforms the national average in growth.

As the beach suit dragged on, I read some of the arguments for and against the beach lawsuit. As a resident of Greenwich, however, I didn't think the town of Greenwich's excellent outside counsel from Hartford was covering the whole rationale for maintaining it as a town park for town residents, owners, and renters alike. I didn't think the town of Greenwich was accentuating the principles of community and sacrifices people make to be part of communities enough. And they clearly were not addressing the "free lunch" part of the equation. This was not surprising as the town's hired attorneys were pressing conventional legal arguments, precedents, and case law, which is the traditional way of proceeding. I wanted to present more than a legalistic argument. I wanted to present why the existing policy was right and how somebody, in my opinion, wanted something for nothing.

As a general matter, in 1998 for one million dollars you could buy a prewar cape house of less than 1,800 sq. ft., with plaster walls, ceilings at 8' or less, one bedroom on the first floor, two bedrooms and one full bath under the eaves on the second floor, and a half bath on the first floor. There was no kitchen/family room. A "normal" person could stand in the musty basement, but I am 6'3" tall, so if I were to stand in the basement, I would have to put my head between the floor joists and avoid hitting my head on plumbing pipes or subsequently installed ductwork for air conditioning. There might be a one-car detached garage that could not fit a Chevrolet Suburban. And you were on .18 to .28 acre. That is what you got for your one million dollars in Greenwich, near Tod's Point.

For that same one million dollars in Stamford, you could get a 1970s builder's special four-bedroom, two-and-a-half-bath home with 8' ceilings on the first and second floors and about 2,800 sq. ft. There would be an actual family room attached to or very close to the kitchen. There would be a full-size, two-car garage attached to the house that could fit a Chevrolet Suburban and some yard tools. You could walk around the basement without hitting your head, and it would not necessarily have that musty smell that can come with old basements. And you might be on a half acre or even an acre. And there was a bonus room above the two-car garage and pull-down stairs for storage in the attic. If you moved into that one-million-dollar Stamford house, you had plenty of room to have three to four kids as they grew up and went off to college or elsewhere after high school. Taxes on the Stamford house would be more than on the Old Greenwich house even though they cost the same. In the one-million-dollar cape in Old Greenwich, you would also dream that maybe one day you could do well enough in your job or both your jobs that you might be able to move up to a house like the one your friend purchased in Stamford for the same amount you paid for your cape. But in return for a smaller house, you got the schools you were seeking, the parks you were seeking, and the train station and local convenience stores. You bought a slightly different lifestyle. Access to Tod's Point definitely factors into the price of real estate in Old Greenwich and Riverside. So to then hear that someone who is enjoying real estate that is much cheaper across the line in Stamford is demanding to have access to the same beach as the cape dwellers sounded like someone asking for a free lunch. The other way to go about it is, if you want to use the beach, then rent a place that gets you to the beach, and be part of the community that made sacrifices to have access to the beach. Don't just bang your fist and say, "Give it to me."

That's the free-lunch part. The other part stemmed from Alexis de Tocqueville's book on America: *Democracy in America*. In 1831 a twenty-six-year-old Frenchman came to America and toured our new democracy. While France had run its horrific revolution after 1789 with the guillotine to chop off your head, mass killings, and demanding new ways of addressing fellow citizens such as *citizen*, the United States was on a different trajectory with her liberty based in law and a bill of rights. De Tocqueville 's *Democracy in America* is a compelling read and identifies what made America special then and still makes her special today. If I had to take one lesson out of that tome, it was that volunteerism and freely formed community organizations were the backbones of our nation. "In the laws of Connecticut, as well as in all those of New England, we find the term and gradual development of that township independence which is the life and mainspring of American liberty at the present day."[36] In Europe your political life began with the upper ranks of society and imperfectly transmitted to the other members of society. "[I]n America, on the contrary, it may be said that the township was organized before the county, the county before the state, the state before the union."[37] While England ran the colonies, there could be no overt government, but instead, "it was therefore obliged to rule secretly in the provincial assemblies, and especially in the townships."[38] It was the "doctrine of the sovereignty of the people [which] came out of the townships and took possession of the state."[39] "The fabric of American empire ought to rest on the solid basis of "The Consent of the People." The streams of national power ought to flow immediately from that pure, original fountain of all legitimate authority."[40]

"The village or township is the only association which is so perfectly natural that, wherever a number of men are collected, it seems

---

[36] *Democracy in America*, p. 40.

[37] Id., p. 40.

[38] Id., p. 56.

[39] Id.

[40] Alexander Hamilton, John Jay, and James Madison, *The Federalist Papers* (New York: New American Library, 1961), no. 22, p. 152.

to constitute itself."[41] "In America not only do municipal bodies exist, but they are kept alive and supported by *town spirit.*"[42] "The New Englander is attached to his township not so much because he was born in it, but because it is a free and strong community, of which he is a member, and which deserves the care spent in managing it."[43] De Tocqueville recognized that towns were very important in New England. As he travelled south, the towns were less important. "The farther we go towards the South, the less active does the business of the township or parish become…" "[T]he public spirit of the local communities is less excited and less influential."[44] Imagine that you came to settle in America, and you go to the woods to start a farm or expand a farm. It was not like France, Germany, or Britain, where French, Germans, and Britons had been farming and cultivating the land for centuries under a feudal system where the king owned all the land. In the United States, the colonizing countries like Great Britain, Holland, Spain, and Portugal spread out and started cultivating new land among indigenous peoples who did not farm on such a large scale. So if you are in the middle of the woods in the Berkshires of Massachusetts or in the Hartford Valley in Connecticut, you could not expect much from the king of England who was an ocean away. You would have to do it yourself, or more importantly, you would have to do it with the help of your neighbors and the local, indigenous peoples. There was the law from England, France, Holland, or Spain that might be the law of your colony, but that did not put food on your plate or a roof over your head. The colonists had to form voluntary groups to govern themselves to prosper. Your town might receive a charter from the capital so that your town could become an official town from what may have started as a trading post for furs and minerals. The colonists came also to experience freedom of religion whether it be Quakers, Puritans, Methodists, Congregationalists, atheists, etc. In Connecticut, you could not have

---

[41] *Democracy in America*, p. 60.

[42] Id., p. 66.

[43] Id.

[44] Id., p. 79.

a town until you had a charter for a Congregational Church. That is how Greenwich started in 1640. That church, my old church, still exists today as the First Congregational Church of Old Greenwich. We called it First Congo. They have a wonderful series of stained glass windows that show pictures of various small structures that served as the meetinghouse for scores of years. It is a beautiful church on the inside and outside. The new settlers did not look to their mother countries to teach them. Instead, these revolutionary citizens believed that an educated citizenry was the best defense of a democracy, whereby a demagogue was less likely to find fertile ground. That is why New England had the highest literacy rate in the world in 1776, not the tired kingdoms of England, France, Spain, or Russia. This was all done at the local level. De Tocqueville marveled at the resourcefulness of the Americans. In France the citizen looks to the king or government to solve their problems. In America, we look to ourselves and our neighbors.

The town of Greenwich had purchased Tod's Point from the Presbyterian Hospital in New York City in 1945 for five hundred fifty thousand dollars and renamed it from Innis Arden to Tod's Point. Since that time the town had been careful to only use town funds to maintain the park. If storms came and damaged the Connecticut shoreline and federal or state money was available to fix things, the town would not take outside-state money to repair damages there. In the winter, between December 1 and March 31, anybody could go there, and it would be open for dogs. So people sacrifice to buy or rent smaller houses or smaller apartments in Greenwich than could be rented outside Greenwich for the same money. Or Greenwich residents paid considerably more to buy the same house than one could buy in neighboring towns in order to buy the intangibles, schools, and Tod's Point to be a part of a community, with its own community organizations, shops, and pulse. If this Stamford attorney really wanted to be part of the community, then he could rent or buy something in town and have unfettered access to Tod's Point.

Ultimately, when I contacted the town of Greenwich's counsel to let them know that I would like to write and submit an *amicus curiae* brief on behalf of the town, they ignored me. They never responded to my writings or phone calls. I reviewed the rules of practice for the superior court, which was the lower-level court before which the case was proceeding, to see how I could file an *amicus curiae* brief, or "friend of the court" brief. It turned out there were no rules at the superior-court level for filing *amicus curiae* briefs. I found rules at the Supreme-Court and appellate-court levels for such briefs, but there were none in the Practice Book for the superior court.

Some years before, while working in New York City, I had participated in a Federalist Society, lawyers' division, *amicus curiae* brief effort when the city's charter was being amended. My job was to get the consent of the other parties to file that brief pursuant to the rules of that New York court. I did that and got the consent of the other parties involved, and then we filed our *amicus curiae* brief, and the side that we were writing for lost. But I was fully familiar with rules of procedure as I worked not only in the courts of Connecticut, but also the courts of the state of New York as well as the federal district courts in the Southern and Eastern Districts of New York and the district of Connecticut. I had even gotten permission to appear in an appeal of a contract claim in Tucson, Arizona, some years before and had another case transferred from the federal court in Connecticut to the federal court in the district of California in Los Angeles, which I continued to work on while the case was in California. They had the most convoluted local rules to supplement the Federal Rules of Civil Procedure, complete with pages that had to have numbers going down the side of each page for easier reference, lest the clerk reject your filing.

Connecticut had no rules at the superior-court level for the filing of *amicus curiae* briefs. And just to translate, an *amicus curiae* brief is Latin for "friend of the court." You are not a party to the action. You are neither the plaintiff nor the defendant, but you want to bring arguments and legal authorities to the attention of the court handling the matter. So I filed my friend-of-the-court brief in March 1998, a twenty-three-page brief with the law clerk's office. In July 1998, the trial-court judge issued an order to show cause on me to appear and argue why I shouldn't be sanctioned under General Statutes sections 51–84 for filing an *amicus curiae* brief without following the rules of practice. Since the order of the judge did not identify a single rule that he believed that I had violated, I wrote the judge on July 15 and pointed out that his notice "does not specify what Rules of Practice are alleged to have been breached. Please notify me before July 22 what rule(s) I am charged with violating so that I may appear and show cause." Prior to July 22, a law clerk for the trial court telephoned me and stated that the trial court would not say what rule(s) the trial court thought had been violated. This is like the State telling you that you have violated a traffic law and that you should come on a particular day to show why you should not be punished for violating a traffic law, and then you ask, "Please tell me which traffic law you think I violated?" And the state says, "No, I won't tell you before or during the hearing."

Under sections 51–84 a court can fine you up to one hundred dollars or suspend or displace your license to practice law. So that is property that the court can take. And if the State can take your property, the requirements of due process kick in. It begs credulity that the State would charge you with violating the traffic laws and then not tell you which one before you appear and argue. I can assure you that whenever I receive a parking ticket on my car in New York City, one of the first things that I do is, I go to the ticket to read the infraction. *What did I do wrong? Was my car in the tow-away zone? Was my car parked in alternate-side-of-the-street parking on the hours that I was not supposed to be there?* You always want to know what you are being charged with.

On July 22, after introducing myself to the judge, I asked again that the judge identify which rules of practice he believed I had violated. Again, he refused and told me to proceed. I then went through the various reasons why a citizen may file an *amicus curiae* brief. Preliminarily, we have the right to petition the government for redress of grievances. We have the Ninth and Tenth Amendments to the Constitution that basically say that those powers not expressly granted to the state and federal government are retained by the people. And although the court would have been well within its rights to set up a procedure for filing *amicus curiae* briefs at the superior-court level, they had chosen not to; therefore, there were no rules on the matter. In addition, an *amicus curiae* is not a party to the action. You do not desire to become a party to the action. And the rules of practice, like most rules of civil procedure, have a catch-all rule that says the rules will be read in the interest of justice. You do not rigidly follow a rule if that perverts justice. And so it went. When I was finally done, the judge declared that he was going to find me guilty of violating Connecticut General Statutes 51–84. Only then did he go through the rules that he believed I had violated. Some of those were based on the false premise that an *amicus curiae* brief filer is a party to the action, which he or she is not. And his penalty was for me to read the entire rules of practice for the superior court and to listen to a Connecticut Bar Association audiotape on the rules of practice—yes, an ignominious end to an effort to do good. But it was a denial of due process since we could not have a hearing to discuss the rules that he believed had been violated during the hearing. If we had actually discussed the rules that the judge believed had been violated, then maybe he would have seen the error of some of his assumptions.

This was the trial court, who was not seeing the due-process violation, but certainly, the Connecticut Supreme Court would see the due-process violation, and the matter could be reheard, and then we could talk about the rules that the judge thought had been vio-lated. I don't hold it against the trial judge for not reading my *amicus curiae* brief, but I do, however, take exception to his refusal to say what rules he believed had been violated before the hearing, not just once, but twice. One should understand that state-court judges in Connecticut do an immense job with their clerks and process an enormous number of civil actions. It verges on heroic, the amount of slip-and-fall cases, car accidents, landlord-tenant, breach-of-con-tract, medical-malpractice, and other cases that get filed every week. And they have to work through them. I will not give you a numbers' breakdown, but their judicial colleagues on the federal bench work on far fewer cases with more personnel and resources per case than the state-court judges.

So what happens when people write to a federal or state judge who is presiding over a case? When cases are before federal- or state-court judges, people sometimes write the judges to express an opinion. Are these people then made parties to the case they are writing on? No. The judges are experienced jurists. What they read could be prejudicial to their unbiased approach to the cases before them. Perhaps, they have law clerks read this unsolicited correspondence before they do? I don't know. But I have seen in the federal system, where a judge received a letter from a citizen and decided the point raised by the citizen was worthy enough to be briefed by the parties and treated the letter as a "motion to *x*, and here is the briefing schedule for the parties to submit research and arguments." This is in the interest of justice, to get it right. Could the trial judge in the beach case have said that he would take the submission of the *amicus curiae* brief as a motion to submit an *amicus curiae* brief and set the deadline for submissions on whether the *amicus curiae* brief should be read rather than seek to penalize a citizen seeking redress of grievances from the government? Well, that didn't happen.

So I appealed the trial court's order to the next appellate court. That appeal was dismissed because "[a]fter this appeal was fully briefed, our Supreme Court decided *State v. Salmon*, 250 Conn. 147,167, 735 A.2d 333 (1999), in which the court clarified that *only an actual party* to the underlying action may file an appeal" (emphasis added). This was interesting because most of the rules that the trial court sanctioned me for were only for parties. And I told the judge that I was not seeking to be a party. So I followed that dismissal with a writ of error directly to the Connecticut Supreme Court. At least the Supreme Court would recognize the violation of due process and allow a new hearing to be held, particularly in view of *State v. Salmon*, which confirmed that I was not a party to the action. And through both the appeal and the writ of error, the attorney general's office of Richard Blumenthal dutifully defended the actions of the superior-court judge in violating the ordinary due-process rights of a citizen and defended a rule that did not exist for filing an *amicus curiae* brief at the superior-court level. Isn't there a story about the king having no clothes? It is not particularly shocking that Attorney General Richard Blumenthal's office defended the lawless action of the lower-court judge as good attorneys advocate for the side that they are representing. An attorney represents the side that they are hired to advocate for. Unfortunately, this should let Connecticut citizens know that Connecticut's own attorney general can be expected to fight hard to uphold the statists' control of Connecticut, whereby the citizen is a subject of the state. And you thought the Revolution had made the citizen the sovereign.

And how did the writ of error go? I lost again. What a surprise that our own Connecticut Supreme Court does not even know basic due process! Before you take somebody's property away or charge them with a violation, you have to tell the citizen specifically which rule they are alleged to have violated. It is like being charged with violating traffic laws, but they never tell you which traffic law was allegedly violated until after they find you guilty. The Supreme Court obfuscated the discussion of due process by referring to a general principle that for deprivation of liberty or property, you "must be accorded adequate notice and a meaningful opportunity to be heard." But they didn't make the connection that a notice that merely orders you to show up on Tuesday and be sanctioned for rules, which they are not going to specify, is not adequate. And a meaningful opportunity to be heard is not one where you have no idea which of the many rules of practice you should be talking about because the judge refuses to identify them before and during the hearing.

At the same time that I was contesting the imposition of penalties, I had gotten a little more than twenty Greenwich residents to sign a petition to submit an *amicus curiae* brief to the Supreme Court on the original beach suit in its appeal to the Connecticut Supreme Court. That motion was submitted with the proposed *amicus curiae* brief attached and followed the rules for *amicus curiae* briefs at the Supreme Court level. On December 5, 2000, the Supreme Court denied permission to submit the brief with one justice dissenting.

They didn't even want to read it. What is the harm in allowing citizens to submit their voices to the government for the redress of grievances? I don't know! Too much justice, perhaps? It could be that our Connecticut Supreme Court has forgotten that the citizen is supposed to be sovereign.

This is the type of Supreme Court who may backstop the special interests that have run Connecticut for special groups of citizens for the past forty years. So if Connecticut voters actually sent sufficient house and Senate members to the General Assembly as well as a governor who were willing to run the state for the benefit of the general citizen under Article 1, Section 2 and not for special groups of citizens like the Hartford Club, this Supreme Court might strike down actions meant to re-institute good government, thereby reaffirming the victory of the State over the citizen.

Chapter 8

Connecticut Supreme Court Denies Constitutional Right to Work with Your Hands and Back to Put Food on Your Plate

IN ANOTHER BOOK on income inequality, I go through the manner in which the administrative state makes life so much more difficult for those who are poor or of lesser economic means by requiring licenses, fees, and other requirements just to work. That the Home Improvement Contractor Act criminalizes a basic human right of working with your hands and back to put food on your plate has escaped the attention of the Connecticut Supreme Court as similar requirements in other states have escaped the notice of their Supreme Courts is shocking! Our Connecticut Supreme Court and lower courts robotically allow property owners to take the materials and labor of laborers if a written home-improvement contract is not existing or if it lacks the necessary verbiage!

Great! "Our hands are tied," they say. They are not. The court is able to speak up for the natural rights of our citizens, *sua sponte*. It may be legal, but it is not right to take the work and sweat from a laborer and prevent him or her from being paid because the statists demand ever more security in documents and disclosures: "You didn't pay an attorney to draft the document for you?" "You didn't get a written agreement?" "Sorry, you, the worker, lose before we even examine whether you should be paid."

The statists oppose increasing the educational choices for the poor, and then the State penalizes the worker when their paperwork is not up to snuff! That does not even count all the many women and men who are dissuaded from even trying to create their own businesses due to the onerous requirements of the State. Every additional requirement stops a few more citizens from trying. And our Supreme Court facilitates the work of the crafty and deft versus the laborer and says the court's hands are tied by the administrative state. We had a revolution for a reason. The citizen is sovereign, not the State. When our Connecticut Supreme Court recognizes that they should be ruling for the citizen in nine-out-of-ten cases between the State and the citizen, unless there is clear and unequivocal language in favor of the State's position, then perhaps, we will be headed back to a constitutional balance as was originally envisioned at our founding, and we will have reclaimed our free will as an independent state.

Returning to the denial of due process by the Connecticut Supreme Court in my *amicus curiae* action, I had filed a motion for reconsideration of their decision at the end of July 2001, which was denied on September 13, 2001, two days after the tragedy of 9/11. Although I could have sought relief in the federal court system, there were much bigger issues after the tragedy of 9/11, so I stopped any further efforts on this task.

Once the decision became final, the disciplinary personnel in Connecticut sent the decision over to the appropriate department in New York State, where I was also admitted to let them know a discipline had been applied to an attorney also admitted in their state. In October 2001, I received a letter from the Departmental Disciplinary Committee of the Supreme Court, Appellate Division of New York State: "Your filing an *amicus curiae* brief without following the rules of practice, may constitute [a violation.]" They received documents and read the Connecticut rules of practice thereafter and came to the same conclusion that I had come to: there are no rules in the rules of practice for filing *amicus curiae* briefs at the Superior Court level. File closed, no action taken.

In the underlying action, the skilled Stamford attorney won the beach suit that Tod's Point was under the public-trust doctrine and that nonresidents could go, but my free-lunch argument won the case. *Plus ça change, plus c'est la même chose!* (The more things change, the more things stay the same!) Yes, nonresidents would be able to go to the beach, but since it costs money to maintain the beach, the nonresident would have to buy a parking voucher for their car and a ticket for themselves. Anybody can still go to the beach for free between December 1 and March 31 or after 5:00 p.m. on other days.

Conclusion

I F THE CONNECTICUT Supreme Court does not even know basic due process, won't even protect a basic human right to work with your hands and back to feed yourself, and is prejudiced in favor of the State, how can we expect them to act if the citizens try to regain constitutional control of the state in the future so that it is run for the benefit of the general citizen under Article 1, Section 2 of the constitution versus for special groups of citizens?

You may live in a state that is run by the statists for the statists. Some states require more workers per 10,000 people than others as a large state like Alaska has a lot of territory and not a lot of people. Perhaps, your states show up here. California is the most populous state and also has the most public workers, which is put at 235,973 state workers. This does not include local and county-level workers, if applicable.[45] Texas has 176,444 state workers. Florida has 111,102 state workers, and then New York State has 179,783 state workers. New York should raise some eyebrows as it has more state workers than Florida and Texas. Both Florida and Texas have more people than New York. The population in July 2019 of these four states were as follows: California, 39,512,223; Texas, 28,995,881; Florida,

---

[45] governing.com, accessed May 5, 2020.

21,477,737; and New York, 19,453,561.[46] The per-capita ratio of state workers to state residents work out to 61 for California, 65 for Texas, 56 for Florida, and 91 for New York.[47] And Connecticut, a compact state with 3,565,287 people, has 115 state workers per 10,000 residents. That is almost double Texas, Florida, and California and even surpasses New York State. But this, in and of itself, is not surprising as Connecticut is matched or exceeded by Alaska, 245 state workers per 10,000 residents; Arkansas, 119; Delaware, 190; Hawaii, 148; Mississippi, 125; Montana, 125; New Mexico, 128; North Dakota, 134; Rhode Island, 117; Vermont, 146; West Virginia, 135; and Wyoming, 160 state workers per 10,000 residents.[48] The question comes back to how much beyond the average pay, health care, and benefits for the private sector does the public sector earn?

Is 42 percent above the national private-sector level, as the Pew Research had shown, fair? And if the Pew Research assumptions are modified and, instead, Connecticut still leads the nation at 33 or 35 percent above the national private-sector average, that is still woeful for the state's general citizens. What if the state's citizens regained control of the state and were able to bring the wages, health care, disability, and pensions back to the *New England Average* of her sister states? Even that average would be above that which is paid by the private sector. But would attaining the *New England Average* bring light at the end of the tunnel? Connecticut has already undermined the generous pensions and health-care benefits promised the public-sector retirees by intentionally underfunding the pensions over decades of budgets. This perfect storm of benefits in excess of Article 1, Section 2 of the Connecticut Constitution, underfunding of pension and health-care obligations, and extremely lackluster performance of the Connecticut economy strangled by the taxes, fees, regulations, revenues, and requirements of the administrative state has thrown Connecticut on the ropes.

---

[46] "List of U.S. States by Population," https://simple.wikipedia.org/wiki/List_of_U.S._states_by_population, accessed May 5, 2020.

[47] governing.com, Id.

[48] Id.

She cannot tax, fee, "new revenue source," "marijuana," or "toll" her way to health. Nonetheless, the Hartford *Chavistas* will champion the latter as an investment in the future of Connecticut. Such course is a surefire suicide by the State as people, businesses, income, capital, and know-how flee the state for more hospitable jurisdictions. Yes, money will still come from New York City to Connecticut via the Gold Coast towns of Fairfield County, but that is all that has staved off the collapse of Connecticut years ago. That golden goose has been killed by this point.

If the Constitution State were run for the benefit of the general citizen under Article 1, Section 2 and pay, at most, the *New England Average* and void unconstitutional emoluments to special classes of citizens and businesses, then Connecticut could save herself. Short of that, the Hartford *Chavistas* will continue to drive the state into an economic ditch and mortgage the future by rolling today's debts and deficits onto future generations, all the while touting their virtue as champions of the poor and middle class.

About the Author

PETER THALHEIM HAS written the recently published *Check "American" and the 2020 Census: Why "American" Should Be the First Category for Your Race, Creed, Color, or Ethnicity* followed by *China, Demise of a Civilization: The Eleven Principles of History and Economics against the Chinese Marxist Model.* This is one in a multiple series of books in the *Life, Love, Liberty* series on domestic and international policies.

Mr. Thalheim is a trained attorney, army reservist, father, home builder, Realtor, former gubernatorial candidate, immigrant, sometimes traveler, and Sunday school teacher.

www.ingramcontent.com/pod-product-compliance
Lightning Source LLC
Chambersburg PA
CBHW051413250726
48655CB00003B/1020